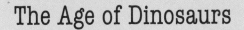

The Age of Dinosaurs

Meet Triceratops WITHDRAWN

Written by Mark Cunningham

Illustrations by Leonello Calvetti and Luca Massini

Cavendish Square

New York

Published in 2014 by Cavendish Square Publishing, LLC
303 Park Avenue South, Suite 1247, New York, NY 10010

First Edition

Website: cavendishsq.com

This publication represents the opinions and views of the author based on his or her personal experience, knowledge, and research. The information in this book serves as a general guide only. The author and publisher have used their best efforts in preparing this book and disclaim liability rising directly or indirectly from the use and application of this book.

CPSIA Compliance Information: Batch #WW14CSQ

All websites were available and accurate when this book was sent to press.

Library of Congress Cataloging-in-Publication Data

Cunningham, Mark.
Meet triceratops / by Mark Cunningham.
p. cm. — (The age of dinosaurs)
Includes index.
ISBN 978-1-62712-607-6 (hardcover) ISBN 978-1-62712-608-3 (paperback) ISBN 978-1-62712-609-0 (ebook)
1. Triceratops — Juvenile literature. I. Cunningham, Mark. II. Title.
QE862.O65 D35 2014
567.915—dc23

Editorial Director: Dean Miller
Art Director: Jeffrey Talbot
Designer: Joseph Macri
Photo Researcher: Julie Alissi, J8 Media
Production Manager: Jennifer Ryder-Talbot
Production Editor: Andrew Coddington

Illustrations by Leonella Calvetti and Luca Massini.

Printed in the United States of America

CONTENTS

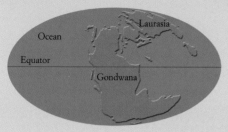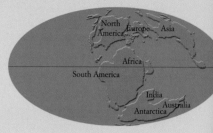

Late Triassic	Early Jurassic	Middle Jurassic
227 – 206 million years ago.	206 – 176 million years ago.	176 – 159 million years ago.

A CHANGING WORLD

Earth's long history began 4.6 billion years ago. Dinosaurs are among the most fascinating animals from the earth's long past.

The word "dinosaur" originates from the Greek words *deinos* and *sauros*, which together mean "fearfully great lizards."

To understand dinosaurs we need to understand geological time, the life time of our planet. Earth history is divided into eras, periods, epochs, and ages. The dinosaur era, called the Mesozoic Era, is divided in three periods: Triassic, which lasted 42 million years; Jurassic, 61 million years; and Cretaceous, 79 million years. Dinosaurs ruled the world for over 160 million years.

4

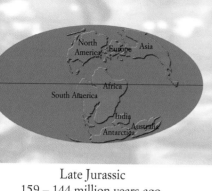
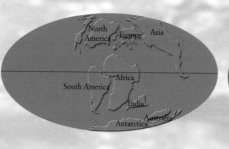

Late Jurassic	Early Cretaceous	Late Cretaceous
159 – 144 million years ago.	144 – 99 million years ago.	99 – 65 million years ago.

Man never met dinosaurs: they had disappeared nearly 65 million years before man's appearance on Earth.

The dinosaur world differed from our world. The climate was warmer, the continents were different, and grass did not even exist!

5

A HORNED GIANT

Triceratops is an Ornithischian dinosaur belonging to a family popularly called ceratopsids. The ceratopsids are known as "horned dinosaurs" because of the horns on their heads.

An adult Triceratops was from 20 to 28 feet (6.1–8.5 m) in length and up to 13 feet (4 m) tall. It weighed about 5.5–6.6 tons (5–6 t). Its body was massive and stocky. Triceratops' enormous head, more than six feet (1.8 m) long, had a wide bony frill above the neck and three horns. There was a long horn just above each eye and a much shorter one on the tip of the snout.

Triceratops' neck frill was bordered by small bony lumps. Scientists think this frill had several jobs. The frill may have intimidated rival males during ritual fighting, and it acted as protection for the neck to avoid serious injuries. Some scientists think the frill helped to cool down Triceratops when their body temperature increased too much. Elephants do the same thing by flapping their wide ears.

FINDING TRICERATOPS

Triceratops was one of the last dinosaurs to populate the earth. It lived in North America about 65 million years ago at the end of the Cretaceous Period of the Mesozoic Era. Remains of Triceratops have been found in Alberta and Saskatchewan (Canada), Montana, North Dakota, South Dakota, Wyoming, and Colorado.

Saskatchewan, Canada

Montana

Wyoming

Colorado

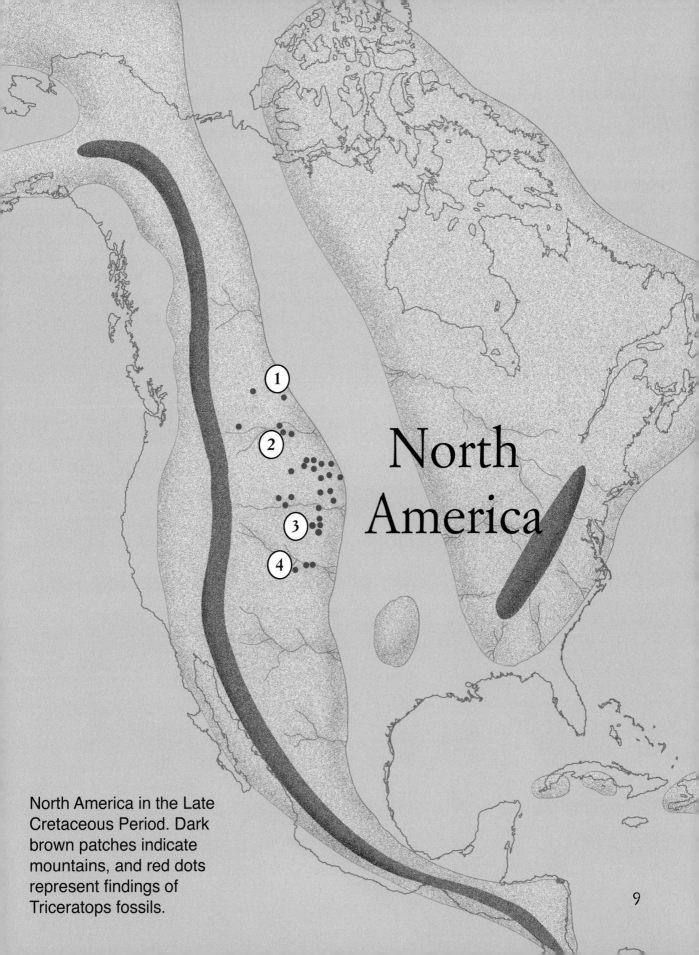

North
America

North America in the Late
Cretaceous Period. Dark
brown patches indicate
mountains, and red dots
represent findings of
Triceratops fossils.

9

BIRTH

Triceratops came into the world from large eggs that the mother laid in a nest. Triceratops was too large and not agile enough to brood, but the mother probably kept watch over the nest to protect the eggs and the hatchlings.

A newborn Triceratops had a very large head, wide eyes, and small bumps instead of horns. Growing, these bumps would become dangerous tools of defense and of attack. However, during the first months of their life, the baby Triceratops were helpless and exposed to all the dangers of a world full of perils.

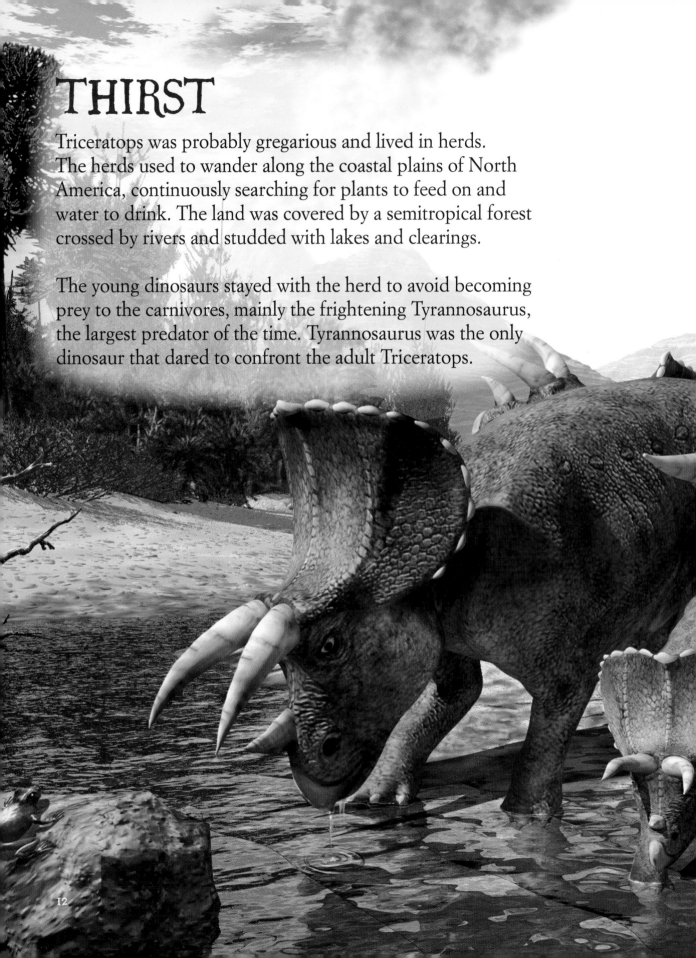

THIRST

Triceratops was probably gregarious and lived in herds. The herds used to wander along the coastal plains of North America, continuously searching for plants to feed on and water to drink. The land was covered by a semitropical forest crossed by rivers and studded with lakes and clearings.

The young dinosaurs stayed with the herd to avoid becoming prey to the carnivores, mainly the frightening Tyrannosaurus, the largest predator of the time. Tyrannosaurus was the only dinosaur that dared to confront the adult Triceratops.

DUELS

Triceratops was not a carnivore, but it was massive and had the ability to attack and defend itself. During breeding season, males had to endure exhausting battles. Two males would fight ritual trials of strength to impress a mate. The entire large skull of these dinosaurs was built in a way to withstand the strong stresses generated when the two males butted heads and locked their horns in an effort to win the battle. Stags, male deer, have these types of battles today.

DEFENSE

More dangerous than ritual fights for mates were the
encounters with large carnivores, above all the fearsome
Tyrannosaurus Rex. The fossil bones of some adult
Triceratops preserve the piercings produced by the teeth of
these terrible predators. The young Triceratops were easier
prey for the predators, and in order to protect them, the
adults would form a defensive circle when attacked.

INSIDE TRICERATOPS

The head of Triceratops was disproportionately large compared to the rest of its body. Its considerable weight was held up by powerful neck muscles. The snout had an enormous nostril and ended with a large hooked "beak," sharp and toothless, like the beak of a parrot.

Teeth were in the back of the mouth and had a strange shape among dinosaur teeth, with a small cutting point and a large two-branched root. These teeth were not numerous and were arranged in layers so that when Triceratops closed its mouth, the rows of teeth acted like the blades of a pair of scissors, able to cut through even the toughest vegetation.

Despite the large size of the Triceratops, its brain was relatively small. Proportionally it was even smaller than that of a modern crocodile. Its sense of smell, however, was relatively well developed.

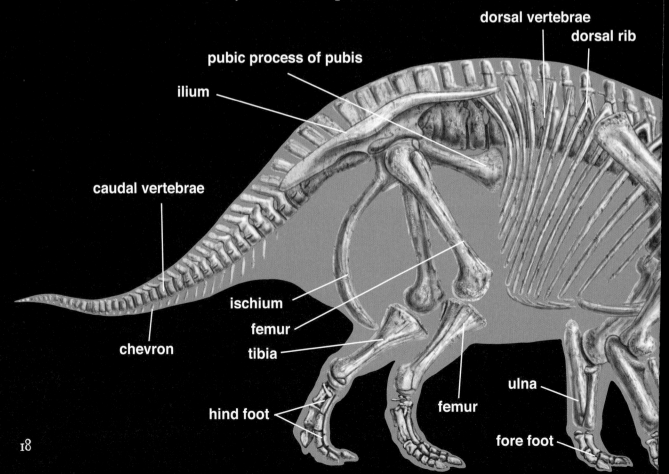

The limbs were strong and stubby to sustain the dinosaur's big body. The fingers and toes were short and ended with rounded little hooves. The forefeet had five fingers and the hind feet had only four toes.

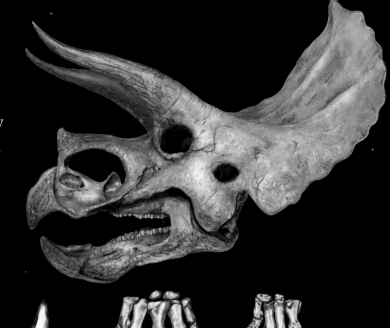

tooth

Left: left forefoot   Right: left hind foot

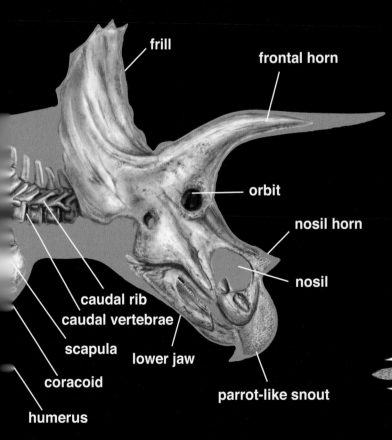

frill

frontal horn

orbit

nosil horn

nosil

caudal rib

caudal vertebrae

scapula

lower jaw

coracoid

humerus

parrot-like snout

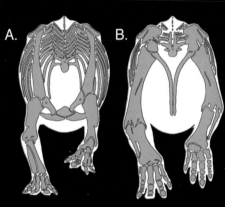

A.   B.

A. Anterior view of skeleton (without neck and skull)

B. Posterior view of skeleton (without tail)

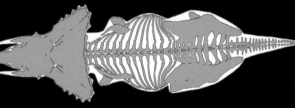

Dorsal view of skeleton

19

FINDING TRICERATOPS FOSSILS

The first fossil remains of Triceratops to be discovered were two long horn cores, found in 1887 near Denver, Colorado. However, they were at first incorrectly identified as fossilized buffalo horns by Charles O. Marsh. In 1889, the dinosaur hunter John Bell Hatcher recovered a nearly complete skull in Wyoming, and Marsh himself named it Triceratops (from the Greek, meaning "face with three horns"). During following years, Hatcher found more than 40 skulls and other bone remains of the large horny dinosaur.

Triceratops is the most common dinosaur to be found in the rocks, dating to the end of the Cretaceous period. To date, at least 50 more or less complete skulls and many other isolated parts of the skeleton, belonging to both adults and young, have been collected.

Most Triceratops fossils collected are the animal's large and massive skull. However, in 1994 two partially preserved skeletons with the bones still in articulation were discovered and excavated in North Dakota. They have been nicknamed "Willy" and "Raymond."

● Torosaurus,
USA and Canada,
65–67 million years ago.

● Pachyrhinosaurus,
Canada and USA
(Alaska), 68–71
million years ago.

Protoceratops,
Mongolia and China,
70–80 million years ago.

THE CERATOPSIDS

The maps show discovery sites of the ceratopsians figured in these pages.

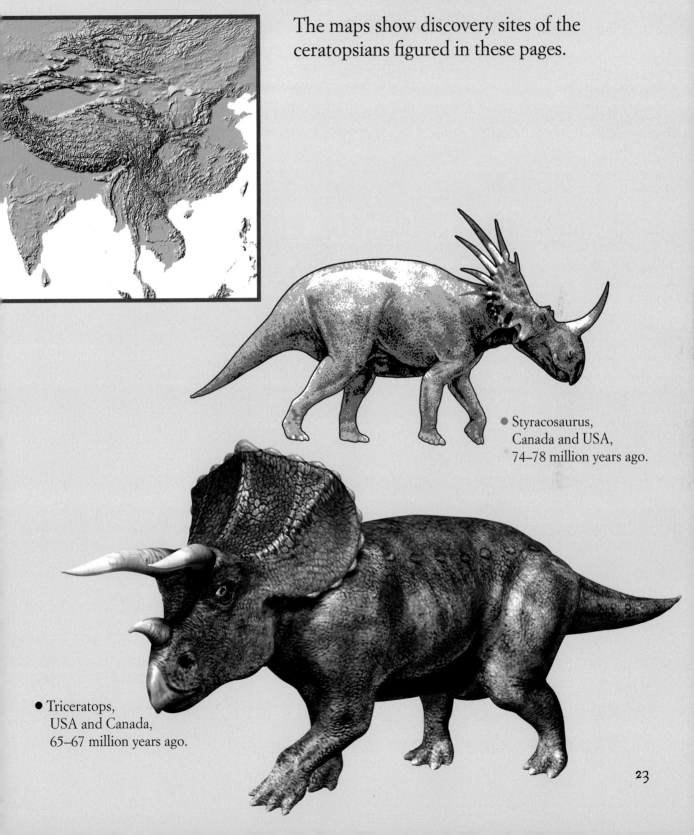

● Styracosaurus,
Canada and USA,
74–78 million years ago.

● Triceratops,
USA and Canada,
65–67 million years ago.

THE GREAT EXTINCTION

Sixty-five million years ago, when Triceratops was the most common large animal in North America, dinosaurs became extinct. Scientists think a large meteorite hitting the earth caused this extinction. A wide crater caused by a meteorite exactly 65 million years ago has been located along the coast of Mexico. The dust suspended in the air by the impact would have obscured the sunlight for a long time, causing a drastic drop in temperature and killing many plants.

The plant-eating dinosaurs would have starved or frozen to death. Meat-eating dinosaurs would have also died without their food supply. However, some scientists believe dinosaurs did not die out completely, and that present-day chickens and other birds are, in a way, the descendants of the large dinosaurs.

A DINOSAUR'S FAMILY TREE

The oldest dinosaur fossils are 220–225 million years old and have been found all over the world.

Dinosaurs are divided into two groups. Saurischians are similar to reptiles, with the pubic bone directed forward, while the Ornithischians are like birds, with the pubic bone directed backward.

Saurischians are subdivided in two main groups: Sauropodomorphs, to which quadrupeds and vegetarians belong; and Theropods, which include bipeds and predators.

Ornithischians are subdivided into three large groups: Thyreophorans which include the quadrupeds Stegosaurians and Ankylosaurians; Ornithopods; and Marginocephalians subdivided into the bipedal Pachycephalosaurians and the mainly quadrupedal Ceratopsians.

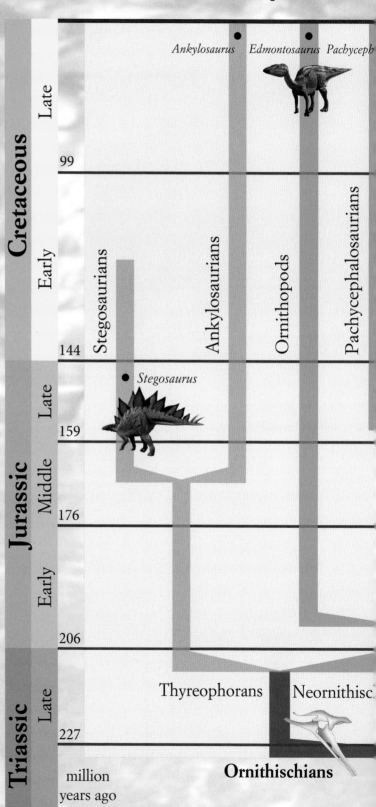

Ankylosaurus Edmontosaurus Pachyceph

Cretaceous — Late / Early — 99 / 144

Jurassic — Late / Middle / Early — 159 / 176 / 206

Triassic — Late — 227

million years ago

Stegosaurus

Stegosaurians Ankylosaurians Ornithopods Pachycephalosaurians

Thyreophorans Neornithisc

Ornithischians

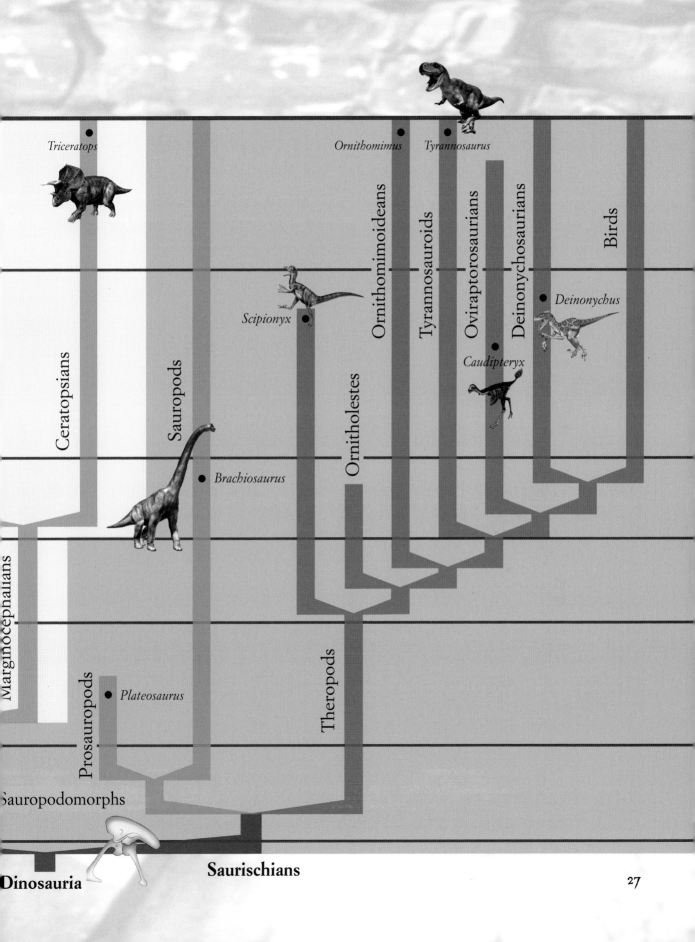

Triceratops

Ornithomimus *Tyrannosaurus*

Ornithomimoideans

Tyrannosauroids

Oviraptorosaurians

Deinonychosaurians

Birds

Deinonychus

Ceratopsians

Sauropods

Scipionyx

Ornitholestes

Caudipteryx

Brachiosaurus

Marginocephalians

Theropods

Prosauropods

Plateosaurus

Sauropodomorphs

Dinosauria

Saurischians

A SHORT VOCABULARY OF DINOSAURS

Bipedal: pertaining to an animal moving on two feet alone, almost always those of the hind legs.

Bone: hard tissue made mainly of calcium phosphate; single element of the skeleton.

Carnivore: a meat-eating animal.

Caudal: pertaining to the tail.

Cenozoic Era (Caenozoic, Tertiary Era): the interval of geological time between 65 million years ago and present day.

Cervical: pertaining to the neck.

Claws: the fingers and toes of predator animals end with pointed and sharp nails, called claws. Those of plant-eaters end with blunt nails, called hooves.

Cretaceous Period: the interval of geological time between 144 and 65 million years ago.

Egg: a large cell enclosed in a porous shell produced by reptiles and birds to reproduce themselves.

Epoch: a division of geologic time.

Evolution: changes in the character states of organisms, species and higher ranks through time.

Feathers: outgrowth of the skin of birds and some other dinosaurs, used in flight and in providing insulation and protection of the body. They evolved from reptilian scales.

Forage: to wander in search of food.

Fossil: evidence of the life in the past. Not only bones, but footprints and trails made by animals, as well as dung, eggs, or plant resin, when fossilized, is a fossil.

Herbivore: a plant-eating animal.

Jurassic Period: the interval of geological time between 206 and 144 million years ago.

Mesozoic Era (Mesozoic, Secondary Era): the interval of the geological time between 248 and 65 million years ago.

Pack: group of predator animals acting together to capture the prey.

Paleontologist: scientists who study and reconstruct prehistoric life.

Paleozoic Era (Paleozoic, Primary Era): the interval of geological time between 570 and 248 million years ago.

Predator: an animal that preys on other animals for food.

Raptor (raptorial): a bird of prey, such as an eagle, hawk, falcon, or owl.

Rectrix (plural rectrices): any of the larger feathers in a bird's tail that are important in helping its flight direction.

Scavenger: an animal that eats dead animals.

Skeleton: a structure of animal body made of several different bones. One primary function is also to protect delicate organs such as the brain, lungs, and heart.

Skin: the external, thin layer of the animal body. Skin cannot fossilize unless it is covered by scales, feathers, or fur.

Skull: bones that protect the brain and the face.

Teeth: tough structures in the jaws used to hold, cut, and sometimes process food.

Terrestrial: living on land.

Triassic Period: the interval of geological time between 248 and 206 million years ago.

Vertebrae: the single bones of the backbone; they protect the spinal cord.

DINOSAUR WEBSITES

Dinosaur Train (pbskids.com/dinosaurtrain/): From the PBS show Dinosaur Train, you can have fun watching videos, printing out pages to color, play games, and learn lots of facts about so many dinosaurs!

The Natural History Museum (http://www.nhm.ac.uk/kids-only/ dinosaurs/): Take a quiz to see how much you know about dinosaurs or a quiz to tell you what type of dinosaur you'd be! There's also a fun directory of dinosaurs, including some cool 3D views of your favorites.

Discovery Channel Dinosaur videos (http://dsc.discovery.com/video-topics/other/dinosaur-videos): Watch almost 100 videos about the life of dinosaurs!

Dinosaurs for Kids (www.kidsdinos.com): There's basic information about most dinosaur types, and you can play dinosaur games, vote for your favorite dinosaur, and learn about the study of dinosaurs, paleontology.

DinoNet (www.dinonet.net): Get the latest news on dinosaur research and discoveries. This site is pretty advanced, so you may need a teacher's or parent's help to find what you're looking for.

MUSEUMS

Yale Peabody Museum of Natural History, 170 Whitney Avenue, New Haven, CT 06520-8118

American Museum Natural History, Central Park West at 79th Street, New York, NY 10024-5192

The Field Museum, 1400 So. Lake Shore Drive, Chicago, IL 60605-2496

Carnegie Museum of Natural History, 4400 Forbes Avenue, Pittsburgh, PA 15213-4080

National Museum of Natural History, the Smithsonian Institution, 10th Street and Constitution Avenue NW, Washington, DC 20560-0136

Museum of the Rockies, 600 W. Kagy Boulevard, Bozeman, MT 59717

Denver Museum of Nature and Science, 2001 Colorado Boulevard, Denver, CO 80205

Dinosaur National Monument, Highway 40, Dinosaur, CO 81610

Sam Noble Museum of Natural History, 2401 Chautauqua, Norman, OK 73072-7029

Museum of Paleontology, University of California, 1101 Valley Life Sciences Bldg., Berkeley, CA 94720-4780

Royal Tyrrell Museum of Palaeontology, Hwy 838, Drumheller, AB T0J 0Y0, Canada

INDEX

Page numbers in **boldface** are images.

....